PUBLIC LIB W9-CLB-964

UNDERSTANDING
OUR
HEAD

LUCY BEEVOR

capstone

© 2017 Heinemann-Raintree
an imprint of Capstone Global Library, LLC
Chicago, Illinois

To contact Capstone Global Library please call 800-747-4992, or visit our web site www.capstonepub.com
All rights reserved. No part of this publication may be reproduced or transmitted in any form or by any
means, electronic or mechanical, including photocopying, recording, taping, or any information storage
and retrieval system, without permission in writing from the publisher.

Edited by Brenda Haugen
Designed by Russell Griesmer and Jennifer Bergstrom
Original illustrations © Capstone Global Library Limited 2016
Picture research by Jo Miller
Production by Jennifer Bergstrom
Originated by Capstone Global Library Limited

20 19 18 17
10 9 8 7 6 5 4 3 2

Library of Congress Cataloging-in-Publication Data
Names: Beevor, Lucy, author.
Title: Understanding our head / by Lucy Beevor.
Description: North Mankato, Minnesota : Capstone Press, [2017] | Series: Raintree perspectives. Brains,
body, bones! | Audience: Ages 8-11. |
  Audience: Grades 4 to 6. | Includes bibliographical references and index.
Identifiers: LCCN 2016036104|
ISBN 9781410985804 (library binding) |
ISBN 9781410985842 (paperback) |
ISBN 9781410985965 (eBook PDF)
Subjects: LCSH: Head—Juvenile literature. | Skull—Juvenile literature. | Brain—Juvenile literature. | Human
anatomy—Juvenile literature.
Classification: LCC QM535 .B427 2017 | DDC 611/.91—dc23
LC record available at https://lccn.loc.gov/2016036104

Acknowledgments
We would like to thank the following for permission to reproduce photographs: Capstone Studio: Karon
Dubke, 27; Dreamstime: Shubhangi Kene, 19; Newscom: EPA/Achim Scheidemann, 20; Shutterstock:
Alila Medical Media, 9, AridOcean, 29 (right), Arthito, 7, Gang Liu, 8, Gleb Semenjuk, 13, GrsphicsRF, 22,
ImagePhoto, 15, Jesada Sabai, 23, Mopic, 14, naluwan, 29 (left), NorGal, 11, Ocskay Bence, 17 (bottom),
oliveromg, 25, Pashin Georgiy, 17 (top), progressman, 7, S K Chavan, 24, Sebastian Kaulitzki, cover,
XiXinXing, 5; design elements: Shutterstock: anyaivanova, designelements, PILart, Ohn Mar, Ri, Studio_G

Every effort has been made to contact copyright holders of material reproduced in this book. Any omissions
will be rectified in subsequent printings if notice is given to the publisher.

All the internet addresses (URLs) given in this book were valid at the time of going to press. However, due
to the dynamic nature of the internet, some addresses may have changed, or sites may have changed or
ceased to exist since publication. While the author and publisher regret any inconvenience this may cause
readers, no responsibility for any such changes can be accepted by either the author or the publisher.

Printed and bound in the USA
052017   010551RP

THE HUMAN HEAD

Look at your face in a mirror. What's the first thing you see? Maybe it's your eyes, nose, or skin. You might think of these features as separate parts. In fact, each of these parts makes up the human head, and they all work together. The mouth is part of the respiratory system because it helps you to breathe. It's also part of the digestive system because it helps you to eat.

These systems are controlled by one amazing organ in your head: the brain. The brain is the most powerful and complex computer that exists. It is a living control room. It controls the work that all the other parts of your body do. Without it, you would not be able to see, hear, smell, taste, or move. It is what makes you alive.

There is a lot going on inside our heads. Scientists still don't fully understand how the brain works.

ON THE SURFACE

You've probably looked at yourself in the mirror thousands of times. But take a closer look. Have you ever noticed all the different things on the surface of your head? From your hair to your pores, they all have important parts to play.

Skin: Magic Material

Imagine a material that is both flexible and strong. If it tears, it repairs itself. It's waterproof, and it controls temperature. This material is your skin, and it's busy. Skin protects you from dirt and germs that could harm your body. The sweat from pores on your skin helps you to keep cool and get rid of waste. And as skin works, it oozes wax and oils that protect it and keep it soft.

Body Talk

Did you know that skin is also an *organ*? In fact, it is the biggest organ in your body.

Did you know that curly hair grows from oval-shaped follicles? Straight hair grows from circular follicles.

follicle

Hair Everywhere!

Take a closer look at the skin on your face. Can you find a spot that isn't covered in hair? Your cheeks? Guess again. Fine hair covers most of your skin, even your cheeks. Skin is pierced by thousands of tubes called hair follicles. Your scalp alone has about 100,000 hair follicles. Your hair may be curly, straight, black, brown, blond, or red. But no matter what it looks like, hair keeps your head and body warm and protected.

The Eyes: Seeing Light

We wouldn't be able to see the world around us without our eyes. When you look at something, what you are actually seeing is light bouncing off that object. Your eyes then turn these light rays into images your brain can understand.

Light travels on an amazing journey through your eyes. First, eyes focus the light. Next, they take a picture, sort of like a camera does. Then they then send information about the picture to your brain.

There are six muscles that attach to your eye. These muscles move your eyes around, up and down, and side to side.

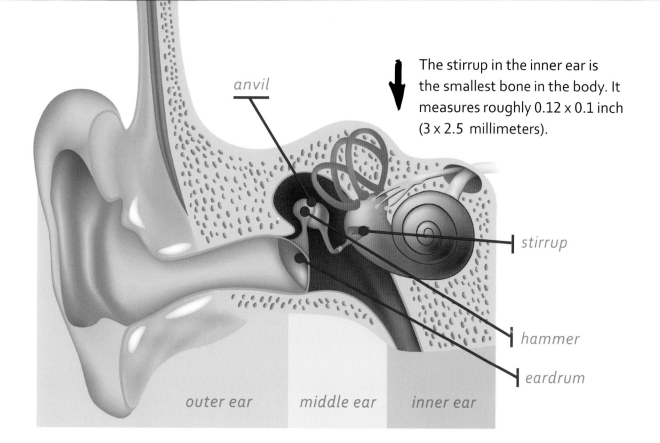

The stirrup in the inner ear is the smallest bone in the body. It measures roughly 0.12 x 0.1 inch (3 x 2.5 millimeters).

anvil

stirrup

hammer

eardrum

outer ear

middle ear

inner ear

The Ears: Hearing Sound

Like your eyes, your ears are also part of an amazing journey. When you hear a sound, you're hearing sound waves. The sound waves are collected by your outer ear and sent through the ear canal. In the middle ear, sound waves vibrate the **eardrum**. The vibration moves three little bones, called the hammer, anvil, and stirrup. These bones send the vibrations on to the inner ear. Tiny hair-like structures called cilia send the vibrations as messages to the brain.

What's in a Name?

The stirrup bone's proper name is the stapes. It gets its nickname because it looks like a tiny stirrup, the metal loop attached to a horse's saddle that holds a rider's foot.

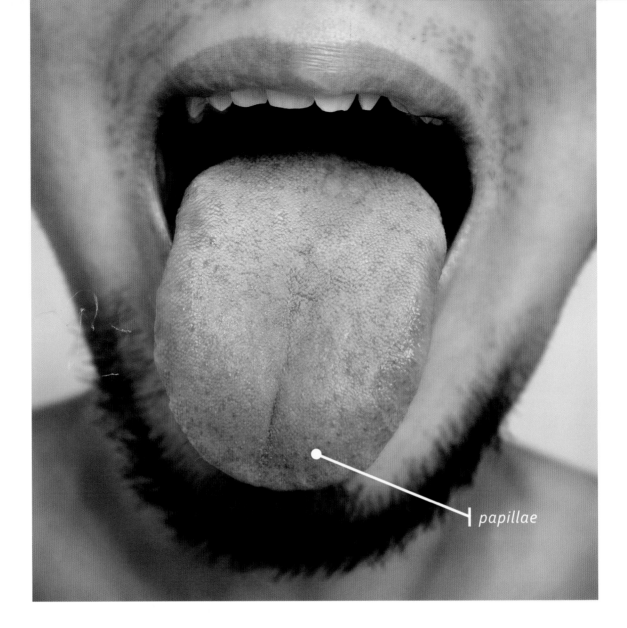

papillae

The Mouth: A Multitasker

For a peek inside the human head, all you have to do is open your mouth. You'll see your tongue and teeth. But it's the parts you can't see that make the mouth's work possible.

 The human tongue has eight muscles. The muscles move our tongues, which helps us to speak.

Saliva pours into your mouth from *glands* below the back teeth and under the tongue. Saliva makes it easier to chew food and to speak. Just think of how hard it is to talk when your mouth is dry.

Sense of Taste

Hidden in the little bumps on your tongue are about 10,000 taste buds. These tiny organs respond to tastes such as sweet, salty, sour, and bitter. Taste buds send messages to the brain about how something tastes. But taste buds only respond to liquid. Dry food in a mouth with no saliva would have no taste at all. Even if you were to place a piece of lemon on a dry tongue, you would not be able to taste that it is sour.

See for Yourself

Look in a mirror and stick out your tongue. Do you see the red bumps on your tongue? They are papillae. Inside the papillae are thousands of taste buds. Amazingly, taste buds are replaced every two weeks.

Body Talk

Like your skin, the *membrane* on the inside of your mouth is strong. It can stand a lot of wear and tear, such as when you bite the inside of your cheek.

The Nose: A Gatekeeper

You can also look inside your nostrils. But there are thousands of **cells** deep inside your nose that you can't see. These cells react to chemicals coming off things that smell, such as a spicy food or freshly baked bread. The cells send messages to your brain about the way a spicy food or a loaf of bread smells.

The nose also plays an important role in keeping us safe. It alerts us to dangerous smells, such as smoke, gas, or food that has gone bad.

See for Yourself

As you eat your lunch, try holding your nostrils closed. Can you still taste the food in your mouth? Even though your mouth is working hard to chew the food, you can't taste it. This is because the nose and the mouth work as a team to help us taste what we eat.

Body Talk

Humans can recognize about 10,000 smells.

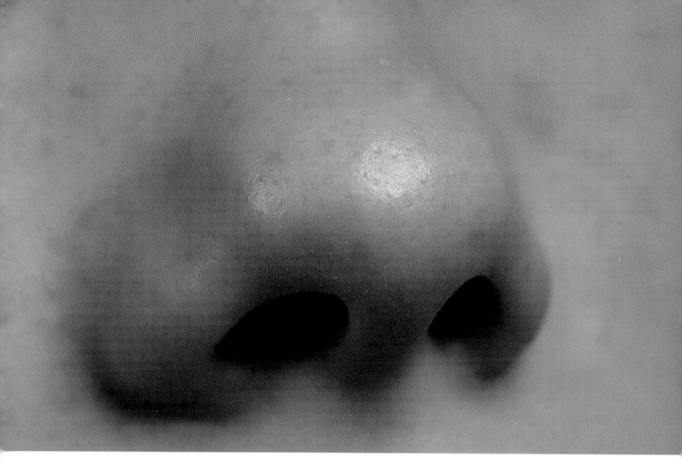

↑ Our noses help us to taste food by sending "smell" signals to the brain when we eat.

Yet 95 percent of the nose plays no role in smelling. Your nose's biggest job is to filter the air you breathe. The nose traps dust and bacteria in slimy mucus. You swallow the mucus to keep the dust and bacteria away from your lungs. Even when we breathe through our mouths, our nose is taking in air. In fact, humans mostly breathe through their noses.

THE NEXT LAYER

Just beneath the skin on your face, there are lots of body parts you couldn't do without. Smiling and talking would be impossible without them. The muscles and bones in our heads are always busy.

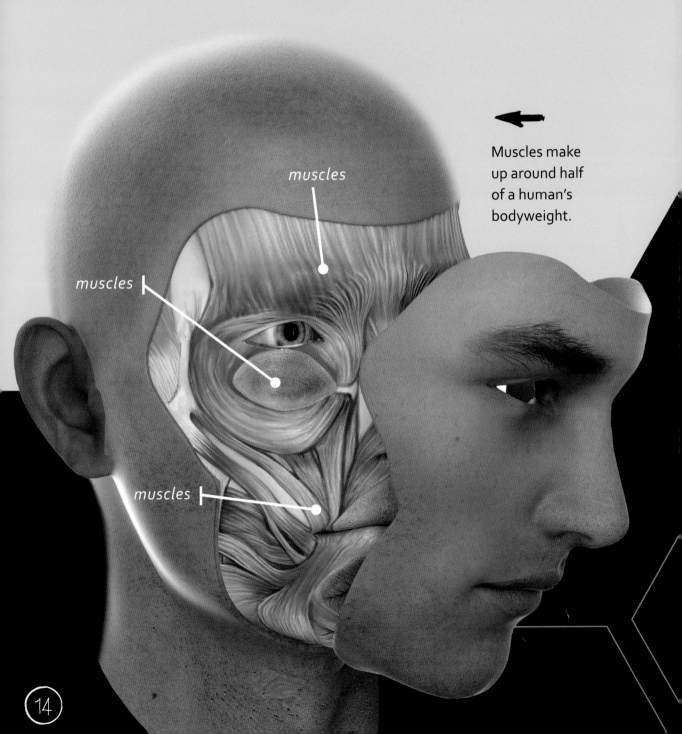

Muscles make up around half of a human's bodyweight.

muscles

muscles

muscles

The Constant Work of Muscle

The human face is constantly moving, from blinking and winking to speaking and chewing. If you could look through your skin, you would see the stretchy muscles that make this movement possible. Muscles can only pull a bone. They can't push. Muscles work in pairs so you can move a body part in more than one direction.

Movement in your face happens more often than you might think. Your eye muscles move about 100,000 times each day. Your face alone has more than 30 muscles! Sometimes you move these muscles on purpose, such as when you make a funny face. But other movements, such as blinking, you don't even think about.

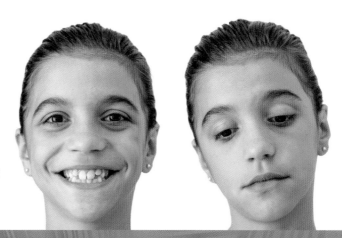

The muscles in the face are working all the time. Without them, you wouldn't be able to smile or frown.

Body Talk

The average person blinks 15 times every minute. Blinking washes tears over our eyes. The tears kill bacteria and help to keep our eyes clean.

Bones: Living Armor

You skull protects your brain and other parts of your face. It is made up of 29 bones. The bones are connected like the pieces of a jigsaw puzzle. The 14 bones of the face are shaped to protect different parts of the head, such as your eyes and nose. These bones are stronger than concrete, yet light enough so that you can still lift your head.

While the skull is like a built-in helmet for your head and face, it is also movable and constantly working. Bones are living organs. Each bone creates blood cells in its soft, spongy center, called the **marrow**.

See for Yourself

Place your fingertips on the area just in front of your ears, and open and close your mouth. Can you feel something moving in and out? That is your jawbone working! The jawbone is the only bone in the skull that moves.

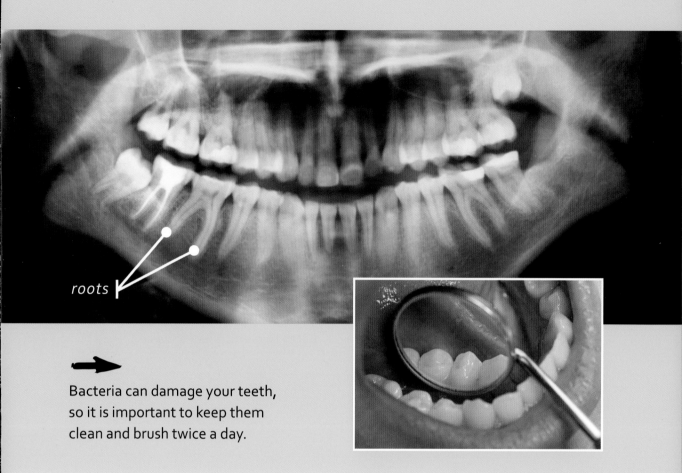

roots

Bacteria can damage your teeth, so it is important to keep them clean and brush twice a day.

Teeth

Just like your bones, your teeth are alive. Inside your teeth is a soft material called pulp. Pulp carries blood that feeds your teeth, keeping them healthy. Pulp goes all the way to the tooth's root. The roots attach firmly to the jawbone so that you can bite and chew at mealtimes.

Blood: Food for Your Head

A network of blood vessels runs all over the muscles and bones of your head. The vessels are tiny tubes, through which the heart pumps oxygen-rich blood to every part of your head. Muscles and organs, such as your brain, need this oxygen to survive.

Strung together, all the blood vessels in your body could circle Earth two and a half times.

See for Yourself

Arteries are a type of blood vessel. The carotid arteries supply blood to your head. Put your fingers on either side of your neck just below your chin. You can feel the carotid arteries pulse as blood flows through them on its way to your head.

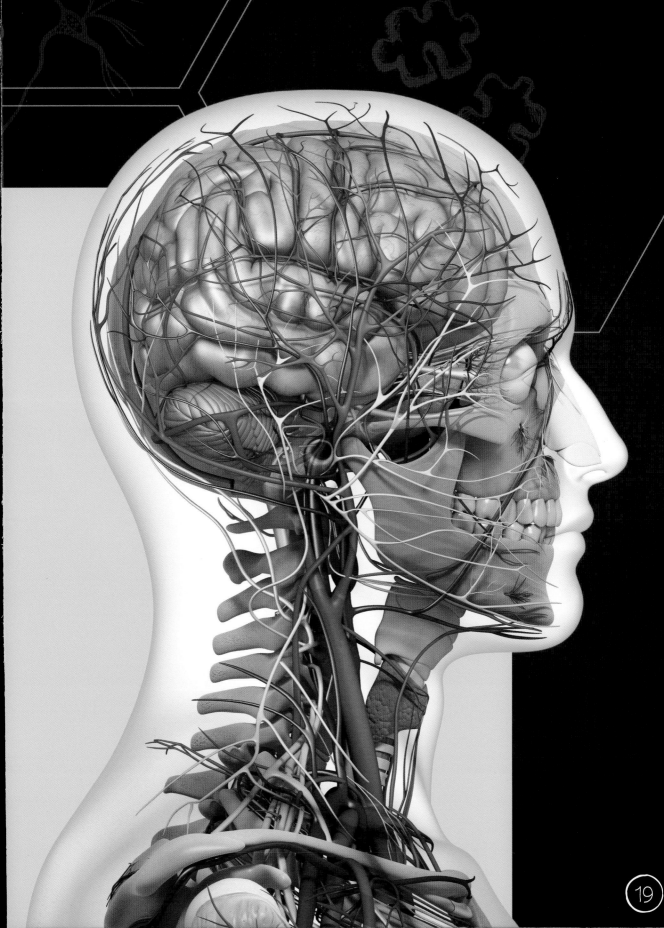

THE BRAIN: A LIVING COMPUTER

The parts of your head would be of little use without one big organ called the brain. The brain is part of the nervous system, which controls everything you do. The nervous system also includes the **spinal cord** and a network of **nerves** throughout your body. Nerves in your hand tell your brain when you touch a hot stove. Your brain answers by pulling your hand away from the heat. Your nervous system also controls breathing and other movements you make without thinking.

Brain Injury

Much of what we know about the brain comes from studying brain injuries. Olympic rower James Cracknell was cycling across the United States when he was hit by a truck in 2012. Cracknell was wearing a helmet, but his head injuries were so bad that he was not expected to live.

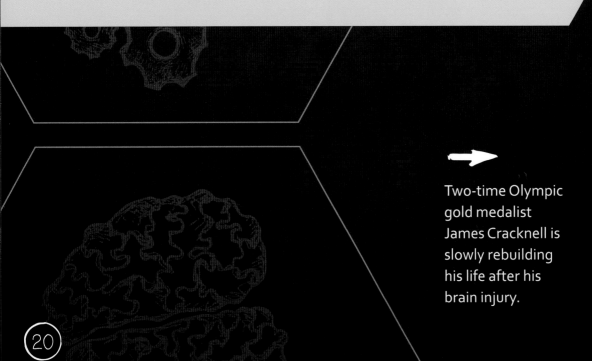

Two-time Olympic gold medalist James Cracknell is slowly rebuilding his life after his brain injury.

Against the odds, Cracknell managed to survive But, his brain was badly damaged, and his personality changed. Cracknell lost his senses of taste and smell and still struggles with his memory. However, with help from his doctors, Cracknell has made great progress since his injury. He has regained his confidence and his physical fitness. His sister-in-law even says that since his injury, he is more talkative and funny. Scientists have learned that injuries to specific parts of the brain affect personality and behavior.

James Cracknell

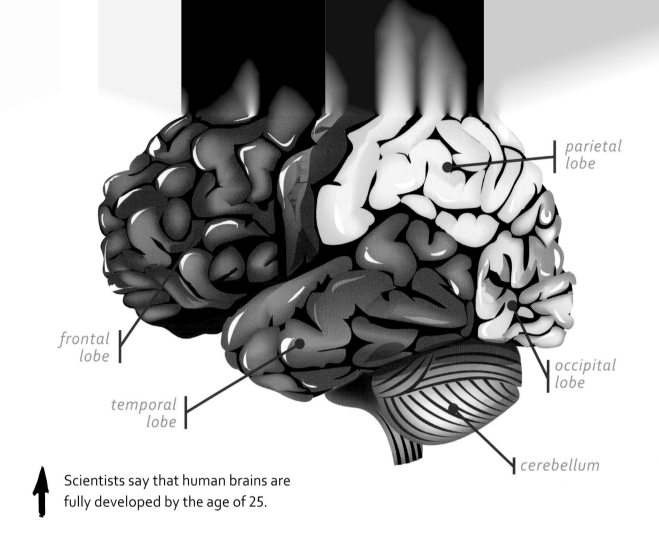

parietal
lobe

frontal
lobe

temporal
lobe

occipital
lobe

cerebellum

Scientists say that human brains are
fully developed by the age of 25.

Bumpy, Lumpy Brain Parts

Your brain is a machine that is made of several parts.
The biggest part is the cerebrum. The cerebrum is
divided into four sections called lobes. Each lobe has
an important job. When you make a decision or feel
an emotion, that's the work of the frontal lobe. The
parietal lobe understands information, such as taste
and temperature. Memory and learning take place in
the temporal lobe. And the occipital lobe helps you
understand what you see.

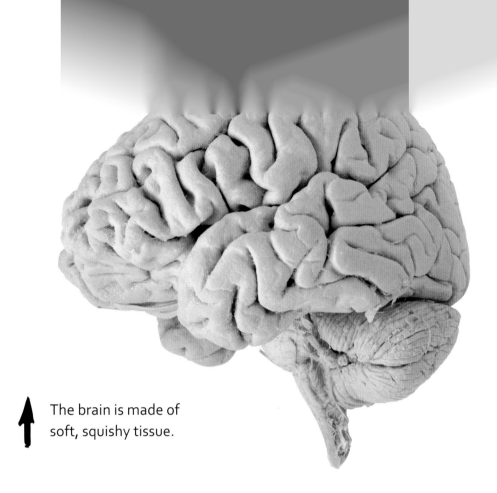

The brain is made of soft, squishy tissue.

The second-largest part of your brain is called the cerebellum. This part is near the back and bottom of your brain. When you use your eyes, legs, and arms to kick a ball or jump up and down, you can thank your cerebellum. It coordinates your body's movement and balance.

Body Talk

The brain floats in a clear, colorless liquid called cerebrospinal fluid. The liquid acts as a cushion in case a person hits his or her head. It is also a barrier to infections and filters out waste. Doctors can check this fluid to look for diseases that may affect the rest of the body, such as *multiple sclerosis*.

The Brain Stem

Messages between your brain and body travel through the brain stem. This bundle of nerves is located at the base of the brain. The brain stem connects the brain to the spinal cord. The spinal cord helps deliver the brain's messages to all parts of the body.

But the brain stem is more than a message center. It controls the activities you need to stay alive, including your heart rate and breathing. The brain stem also controls when you sleep.

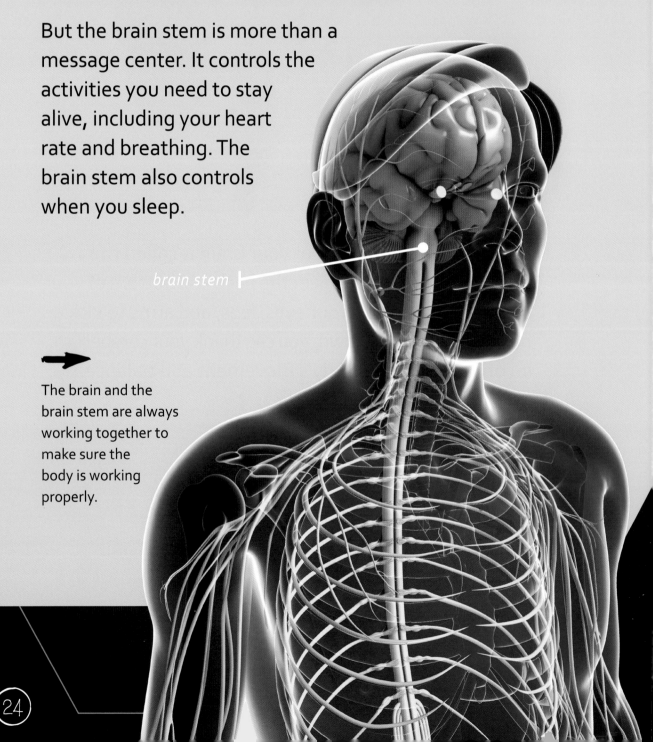

brain stem

➡

The brain and the brain stem are always working together to make sure the body is working properly.

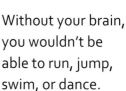

Without your brain, you wouldn't be able to run, jump, swim, or dance.

Brain Power

Your body is constantly moving. You run with your legs and speak with your mouth. Your stomach helps you to digest food. But it is your brain that makes you alive. For example, your eyes do a lot of work to focus light. But it's the brain that actually sees. Think about when you race your friend on the playground. It's your brain that tells your legs to move.

Body Talk

Nerves branch out to connect all parts of the body to the brain. The human brain contains more than 100 billion nerve cells called neurons.

ALWAYS WORKING

The human brain is constantly active. This activity includes sound traveling through the ears, blood rushing through the arteries, and messages moving through the nervous system. The brain understands each message and responds as needed.

Even while you're reading this book, the muscles of your face are moving. Your eyes focus the light that allows you to see the words. Your ears receive the sounds all around you. Meanwhile, your salivary glands are busy responding to the smell of food picked up by your nose. The human head is an amazing combination of the systems at work in the busy machine that is your body. You'd really be lost without your head!

Did you know your brain is 73 percent water? That's one of the reasons why it's important to stay hydrated.

A — **SKIN** Skin can be either thick or thin. The thinnest skin is on your eyelids.

B — **EYES** Your eye lens sits just behind the iris, which is the colored part of the eye.

C — **NOSE** The tiny, stiff hairs in your nose help to keep dust and dirt out of your lungs.

D — **MOUTH** Glands in your mouth make about 3 pints (1.4 liters) of saliva every day.

E — **TEETH** Tooth enamel is strong, but acids from bacteria in your mouth can eat a hole right through your teeth.

F — **BRAIN** The brain contains more than 10 billion nerve cells.

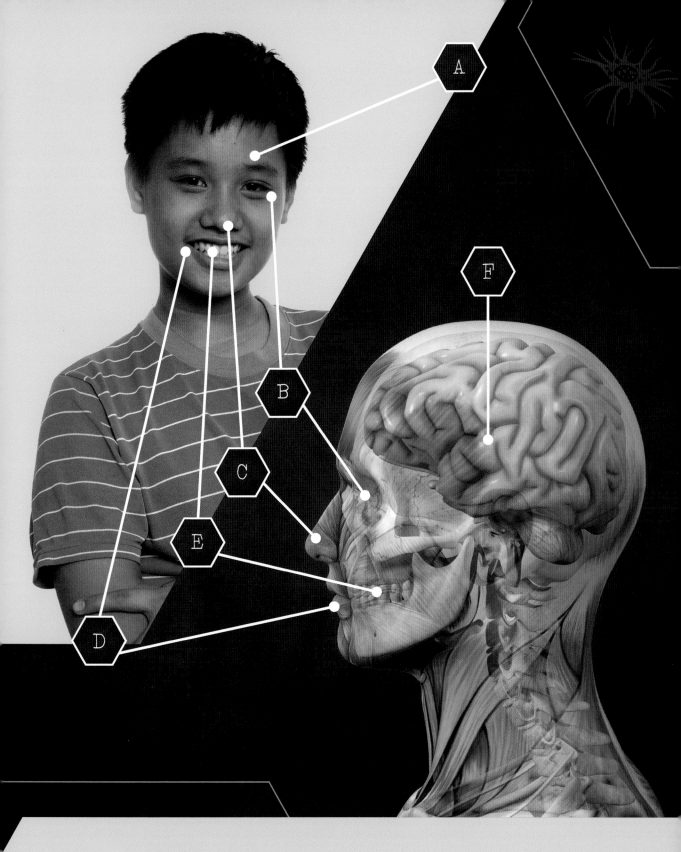

GLOSSARY

artery (AR-tuh-ree)—large blood vessel that carries blood away from the heart

cell (SEL)—smallest structure in the body; different types of cells do different jobs

eardrum (EER-druhm)—thin piece of skin stretched tight like a drum inside the ear; the eardrum vibrates when sound waves strike it

gland (GLAND)—organ that either produces chemicals or allows substances to leave the body

marrow (MA-roh)—soft substance inside bones where blood cells are made

membrane (MEM-brayn)—soft lining in the body; skin is a kind of membrane

mucus (MYOO-kuhss)—sticky liquid that coats the inside of the nose, throat, and mouth

multiple sclerosis (MUHL-tuh-puhl skluh-ROH-suhss)—disease that can affect the brain, spinal cord, and nervous system

nerve (NURV)—thin fiber that sends messages between your brain and other parts of your body

organ (OR-guhn)—part of the body that has a particularly important job, such as your heart or brain

pore (POR)—one of the tiny holes in your skin through which you sweat

saliva (suh-LYE-vuh)—clear liquid in your mouth that helps you swallow and begin to digest food

spinal cord (SPYE-nuhl KORD)—thick cord of nerve tissue in the neck and back; the spinal cord links the brain to the body's other nerves

tissue (TISH-yoo)—collection of cells that makes up the body; tissues perform different actions

READ MORE

Brown, Carron, and Rachael Saunders. *The Human Body*. Shine-a-Light. Tulsa, Okla.: Kane Miller Books, 2016.

Wilsdon, Christina, Patricia Daniels, and Jen Agresta. *Ultimate Body-Pedia*. Washington, D.C.: National Geographic Kids, 2014.

Winston, Robert. *What Goes on in My Head?* New York: DK Children, 2016.

INTERNET SITES

FactHound offers a safe, fun way to find Internet sites related to this book. All of the sites on FactHound have been researched by our staff.

Here's all you do:

Visit *www.facthound.com*

Type in this code: 9781410985804

 Check out projects, games and lots more at **www.capstonekids.com**

INDEX